DR. THOMAS G. O'BRIEN II

MEDICAL MARIJUANA

Real-life success stories

BY

DR. THOMAS G. O'BRIEN II

121 East 60th Street, Suite 4D

New York, New York 10065

(212) 201 - 9122

www.DocTommyO.com

Ordering Information: Quantity sales. Special discounts are available on quantity purchases by corporations, associations, and others. Orders by U.S. trade bookstores and wholesalers.

DREAMSTARTERS

www.DreamStartersPublishing.com

Table of Contents

Introduction

Allow me to introduce myself. My name is Dr. Thomas G. O'Brien II and I am a family physician who specializes in the field of Medical Marijuana. The purpose of this book is so you, as the reader, can get an understanding of the health benefits of Medical Marijuana.

Since receiving my degree in Osteopathic Medicine in 1995, I've devoted my life to helping and educating individuals so that they can take control of their well-being. Within the scope of my practice, not only do I treat a wide variety of health conditions, I also treat a wide variety of individuals who vary in age, race and life experience. I've worked with patients; from young to old, rich to poor, famous to just "regular folks". What they all have in common is that they simply *"don't feel well."* They see the "check engine light" for their body illuminated, and realize they shouldn't ignore it. They are in chronic pain and/or are suffering from a severe illness and are looking for, not only relief, but compassion. They feel alone in their struggle, until they enter my office.

When talking to my patients, I break down complex medical conditions and treatments in a way that they can understand so they can make the best decisions regarding their health. My approach to medicine is integrative in design. I blend a variety of treatments and medications, both natural and conventional, to bring out maximum health for each individual.

Every patient is unique, and I look at each as an individual who needs a personalized approach to their health plan. It's just not enough to treat symptoms; I look at the mind, body, and spirit of each and every person receiving treatment in my office. My broad background as a Family Physician gives me a global understanding of human health, versus a specialist who only looks at one specific part of the body. As a result, I'm able to treat more than one condition at a time and see the connections of various symptoms.

At my office, I conduct an in-depth interview (history) and a thorough physical exam, to help understand what a person is suffering from to get to the root cause. During that first office visit, I look at them, I listen to them, and I feel them both physically and emotionally. Illnesses are not only physical but emotional as well. During the history and physical of an individual, I ask myself the following questions:

What is the patient's mindset?
What are they going through emotionally?

This holistic approach to health, and how I interact with my patients, enables me to explore a variety of treatment strategies to maximize a patient's well-being.

Medical Marijuana

Since I look at the patient as a complete person with a mind, body and spirit, I can do much more for them than just simply doling out pills. If a patient is feeling incomplete in any of those three aspects, finding a healthy balance will be difficult. An individual needs to feel strong in all three aspects to maximize their well-being.

As a child, my parents instilled in me not only the value of working hard to achieve my goals, but to be truly successful, you must also live your life as a caring, compassionate and thoughtful individual. These traits have always served me well in my work. In today's world, it is so important for me to make a real connection with my patients so that they are able to feel comfortable in our doctor-patient relationship.

So often, people get wrapped up in the hustle and bustle of everyday life, they forget to slow down and take the time to care for themselves and their medical needs. I impart this sentiment to my patients; making sure they take time for themselves and letting them know that I care, and that I'm here for them, physically and spiritually.

Physically, I am available to my patient's needs, whatever they may entail, 24/7. Whether a problem, or simply a question, my patients have access to me, at all times, to insure they feel secure in their treatment. Spiritually, I talk to them about faith; faith in themselves, faith in me and faith in a higher power. I try to get them to tap into their spiritual energy

6

so they can see their life in a positive light. I help them to see that this spiritual energy can help them through times of pain and suffering.

One day, a patient visited my office. The patient had just learned of a late stage diagnosis of cancer. As I'm listening to the patient, I can see the patient is at their breaking point. The patient starts to cry as they feel the weight of their diagnosis, and what it means in terms of their possibly limited time left in this world. I stood up from my desk and gave the patient a long strong hug. This physical connection allowed the patient to let down their walls and release some of their fears. Then, I said, *"There is always a plan, you must believe in yourself, believe in me, and believe in the future."*

This wasn't the first time, nor the last, that I gave a patient a hug or made a physical connection with a patient to ease their pain. This wasn't the first time, nor the last, I spoke to a patient about faith. This is, and always will be, part of the way I practice medicine. Unfortunately, many others in the medical field omit this important part of treating patients.

Medical Marijuana

Throughout all my years of practicing medicine, I have seen successful therapies, but many of them have potentially harmful side effects. I'm sure all of you have seen pharmaceutical commercials that have a laundry list of side effects associated with them, and which seem scarier than the illness itself. Many feel if the disease doesn't kill you, the cure will! The practice of medicine, in the United States, is traditionally conservative. We move slowly to put forth new treatments and studies.

Here in New York, we are even more conservative, I think, than many other parts of the country. We take a very slow approach instituting new procedures and treatments. In 1996, California became the first state to legalize the use of Medical Marijuana. Subsequently, many states quickly followed suit. However, it was not until July 2014 that New York State legalized the use of Medical Marijuana. At this time, New York passed the Compassionate Care Act of New York which allowed the use of Medical Marijuana to treat a variety of medical conditions: Amyotrophic Lateral Sclerosis (ALS), Cancer, Chronic Pain, Epilepsy, Human Immunodeficiency Virus and Acquired Immunodeficiency Syndrome (HIV/AIDS), Huntington's Chorea, Irritable Bowel Disease (Crohn's Disease and Ulcerative Colitis), Multiple Sclerosis (MS), Neuropathy, Opioid Addiction, Parkinson's Disease, Post-Traumatic Stress Disorder (PTSD), and Spinal Cord Injury.

With the use of Medical Marijuana, I able treat a wide variety of serious medical conditions, with little or no negative side-effects. As one of the first doctors to be certified by the State of New York to prescribe Medical Marijuana, I've had numerous cases where I was able to improve a patient's quality of life significantly. In many cases, it resulted in a reduction of their pain and/or symptoms so they could regain control of their life. While in other cases, it served as a way of just making someone more comfortable in their final moments of life. You may be asking yourself:

Why is he writing this book?
What does he hope the reader will learn?

The answer is, I want to give back to you, the reader, and let you know that, no matter what you're going through in life, there is help and compassion in the world. I want you to have the facts so that you can live a better and healthier life. I want to continue to share my knowledge as I have done previously through my community outreaches, through my non-profit organization, and through my television and radio programs. I want this book to serve as another tool that helps me give back to those in need. I am more than just a physician. I am an educator who wants to make sure that everybody, not only my patients and their families, has an understanding of how the right doctor and the use of Medical Marijuana can improve quality of life.

I cannot diagnose nor treat you through the pages in this book, I can only educate, and that is what this book is designed to do. I will detail how patients who have visited me in my practice have benefited from the use of Medical Marijuana, and how Medical Marijuana works in the body. My job, through this book, is to inform and educate, and let you know that you're not alone.

DR. THOMAS G. O'BRIEN II

NOTICE

This book is not intended to be a substitute for the medical advice of a licensed physician. The reader should consult with their doctor in any matters relating to his/her health and particularly with respect to any symptoms that may require diagnosis or medical attention. Before beginning any new health plan or program, please seek medical advice from your personal physician.

Chapter 1

What is Medical Marijuana?

Many times, when explaining the medicinal uses of Medical Marijuana, people look at me like I'm crazy. You can see in their eyes that their mind has invoked the image of Spicoli, Sean Penn's stoner character from the movie <u>Fast Times at Ridgemont High</u>. **I get it!** Many people, who are unaware of all the benefits, think that Medical Marijuana is used simply as an excuse to get high. But, in reality, it's a powerful medicine and natural supplement that helps support good health in the body and mind.

There aren't that many topics that cause as much debate among politicians, researchers, scientists, doctors, and the general public, than the use of Medical Marijuana.

There are questions on whether it is safe, effective, long term side effects and what conditions it can actually treat and provide health benefits for. Is it really a "miracle" drug, as some people claim? Or Is it just an excuse to legalize the use of marijuana?

The health benefits of Medical Marijuana are well documented, and although I will touch upon various research and case studies, this book is not intended to be a textbook on the research. As the use of Medical Marijuana is relatively new, many questions still remain about what other medical conditions can benefit from its use. To begin the discussion, let's take a step back, and take a closer look at the make-up and medical uses of marijuana, in general.

Within the marijuana plant, there are 400 different chemicals, 70 of them have been shown to have medicinal properties. The two main chemicals used for medicinal purposes are Tetrahydrocannabinol (THC) and Cannabidiol (CBD).

THC is the chemical in marijuana that has psychoactive properties and causes the "stoner's high." CBD is the chemical in marijuana that has anti-inflammatory, anti-spasmatic and anti-angiogenesis properties. None of CBD's properties would lead to a feeling of being "high". With a new CBD-dominant strain that has little, if any at all, intoxicating effects, the medicinal qualities of the marijuana plant can be better utilized. Due to the limited amount of THC in these plants within this CBD-dominant strain, there is very little "high" effect.

Structurally, both THC and CBD look almost identical. However, CBD is lacking one bond which changes the characteristic of the chemical. What this means is THC and CBD have different neurotransmitter receptors. THC has cannabinoid 1 (CB1) receptors, which are primarily found in the central nervous system. CBD has cannabinoid 2 (CB2) receptors, which are found mostly in the gastrointestinal tract, immune system, smooth muscle tissue, and adipose tissue (fat cells). Those fat cells are important, because the chemical can get stored there, and the fat acts as a natural slow release mechanism. As a result, each of these two chemicals will produce different medical benefits.

THC helps with neuropathic pain relief, fights and kills cancer cells, and stimulates appetite as well as works as a sleep aid. CBD benefits include anti-inflammatory, antispasmodic, and anti-anxiety effects, as well as the reduction in dull achy pain. Additionally, CBD has anti-angiogenesis properties which results in the shrinkage and killing of cancer cells.

As of the writing of this book, the use of Medical Marijuana has been legalized in 32 states and Washington, DC. However, in the eyes of the federal government, marijuana, in any form, is deemed illegal. The Obama administration didn't prioritize the prosecution of individuals who were using marijuana for medical reasons. The Trump administration has continued to not interfere with state laws related to Medical Marijuana, although there have been threats to reverse this stance. With all that said, approximately 85% of Americans support legalizing marijuana for medical use, and several million Americans are currently using it.

Reported benefits of Cannabidiol (CBD), a chemical found in the marijuana plant, include relief of anxiety, pain, insomnia, and muscle spasms. Some patients and doctors report that CBD use has helped epileptic seizures, and some emerging evidence indicates that a particular form of childhood epilepsy, called Dravet Syndrome, responds extremely well to a particular CBD dominant strain of marijuana. But, the most common use for medical marijuana in the United States is for chronic pain.

Millions of Americans suffer with chronic pain due to a variety of medical conditions. The appeal of Medical Marijuana, for the use of chronic pain, is how safe it is when compared to the deadly opiates that are causing an epidemic and destroying our country. Medical Marijuana is not known to be associated with addiction and it is almost impossible to cause an overdose.

Medical Marijuana has also been reported, by patients, to ease the pain of multiple sclerosis, as well as nerve pain in general. Patients report that Medical Marijuana helps them resume their previous activity levels, without the highly sedating quality that opiates produce. Similarly, Medical Marijuana has been reported to be a highly effective muscle relaxant and has helped lessen tremors due to Parkinson's disease as well as pain from fibromyalgia, endometriosis and other pain/inflammation cycles.

PTSD has become an overwhelming problem in this country for our active, non-active and retired military personnel. According to research done by the United States Department of Veterans Affair, somewhere between 10-20% of all military personnel are affected by PTSD. With the inclusion of PTSD as a qualifying medical condition for the use of Medical Marijuana, a decrease in associated symptoms of PTSD is being noted.

Medical Marijuana has also been shown to help manage the nausea and weight loss resulting from cancer treatment or other wasting syndromes, like HIV/AIDS, as well as intestinal issues like Ulcerative Colitis and Crohn's disease. The THC chemical in Medical Marijuana helps stimulate one's appetite, while the CBD helps to reduce the nausea the patient might be experiencing. The results are well documented and as more studies are done, the body of evidence continues to grow. All I know, and can accurately state, are the results I see in my office and what my colleagues have reported.

First and foremost, I tell my patients that the goal of the Medical Marijuana treatment is for them to be comfortable, functional, and to improve their quality of life. I begin by asking the patient:

*What is the most important symptom they want
me to address in order to improve their everyday
life? Is it pain? Is it inflammation? Are we going
to try and boost the immune system? Am I going
to help you kill cancer cells? Are you losing
weight due to loss of appetite or nausea? Do you
want to be conservative with your treatment, or
aggressive?*

Once I have the answers to these questions, the patient and I decide on the proper course of treatment. When prescribing Medical Marijuana to my patients, I must develop a protocol using the ratios of THC to CBD that can be prescribed legally in the state of New York. These include a Low THC - High CBD ratio, an equal THC - CBD ratio, and finally a High THC - Low CBD ratio. Each of these ratios has different benefits and limitations, so as a physician, I have to choose what will work best for each patient.

In the State of New York, there are three delivery systems that are available. First, there is a vapor or e-pen, much like the popular e-cigarettes, with an onset of action in about 90-seconds, lasting around three hours. The second delivery system is a tincture, which is a sublingual (under the tongue) drop. Onset of action is about 20 minutes, and this lasts about four hours, depending on the patient's metabolism. Finally, we have gel capsules that take effect after an hour and a half, lasting four to six hours.

In my practice, I believe that it's critical that the patient is involved in the decision-making process of choosing the most beneficial treatment plan. I spend, at a minimum, an hour with the patient to ensure the patient feels comfortable, and understands the treatment plan that we have decided upon. By taking the time to educate my patients, and enrich their understanding on the use of Medical Marijuana, I believe the patient will remain compliant, resulting in a better outcome.

What I will outline with the case presentations in this book is how the prescription and use of Medical Marijuana helped patients with a variety of ailments; from HIV to cancer, chronic pain to IBD. As we go through the case-studies, keep in mind that everyone is different. What works for one, does not work for all. Choosing, and tweaking (if needed) the ratio of THC to CBD, is an important step in determining each individual patient's treatment plan. I hope that by reading through the case presentations, and getting to know some of my patients the way that I have, you will see yourself, or your loved ones, in these pages. This can be a starting point for you to have a conversation with your doctor about the benefits of Medical Marijuana and whether it's the right choice for you.

To maintain HIPPA regulations, names
and identifying details have been changed
to protect the privacy of the individuals

Special thanks to my patients for giving me
permission to use their stories to educate others

Chapter 2

Human Immunodeficiency Virus

This patient lives in upstate New York, a three and a half hour drive from Manhattan, where my office is located. Being one of the first, and at the time few, New York physicians to be certified in treating with Medical Marijuana, the patient heard about me through one of my first patients who was being treated with Medical Marijuana. The patient came to my New York City office just a few weeks after the January 2015 passage of the Compassionate Care Act.

The patient was suffering from associated symptoms of HIV, and had exhausted all conventional western medicine therapies. Medications for HIV are extremely toxic to the body resulting in most people feeling very sick and losing weight. In extreme cases, patients experience displacement of the adipose tissue in their face, called lipodystrophy, causing the patient to look like Skeletor, the fictional character in the cartoon, Masters of the Universe.

In 1987, when AZT was introduced as the first AIDS/HIV medication, it wasn't very effective. Many people still died, and the medication itself, an anti-viral, caused symptoms such as; problems with the immune system, nausea, vomiting, and severe headaches. As the epidemic continued to rage into the mid-1990s, I was fortunate to be trained in The Bronx, New York, which had the highest number of individuals infected with HIV in the United States.

One of my attending physicians was a speaker during the International AIDS Conference, in Vancouver, Canada. He returned from Canada and addressed the family practice residents by saying, *"You guys are going to implement this immediately - this isn't even in print, yet."* He gave us loose pieces of paper that described the now famous "HIV cocktail," that finally showed sustained success for HIV patients. This was in the summer of 1996, and it changed everything!

There are more than 40 medications used for HIV patients, and specific combinations of these medications can extend and save lives. However, in some cases, they can lower a patient's quality of life, and that's why this patient had come to see me. The patient was unable to find a physician upstate to help explore how Medical Marijuana might help improve the patient's quality of life. So, the patient trekked the three and a half hours to Manhattan to visit with me in my office.

The patient arrived, extremely underweight, and experiencing neuropathy (pain and numbness) of the upper and lower extremities. Both of these symptoms are associated with some of the HIV medications, so it's not uncommon to see this in HIV patients. The infectious disease doctor, whose care the patient was under, had added more medications to the patient's current regimen to help reduce the pain. Unfortunately, it was not helping.

The patient continued to lose weight and was worried about what this meant for their overall health and well-being. The medications were making the patient sick, basically causing decreased appetite, hence the weight loss. Don't get me wrong, the patient was alive because of these medications; they were suppressing the virus and supporting the immune system. However, the medications were not stimulating appetite, nor were they providing any pain relief.

After a thorough examination, I found the patient underweight, in extreme pain, but with no signs of the Kaposi sarcoma lesions, the skin cancer commonly associated with AIDS patients. The medications were saving the patient's life, as they were keeping the viral load down and the CD4 count high. Therefore, the secondary infections and cancer that are the hallmarks of AIDS were not emerging.

When deciding how to help the patient, I had to decide what would work best to stimulate appetite and block pain. If I went with the Low THC - High CBD ratio, I could effectively help decrease inflammation, with a reduction of some pain, but get very low appetite stimulation. Using the High THC - Low CBD ratio, one could expect appetite stimulation and pain relief, but low inflammation relief.

So, I chose an equal ratio of THC and CBD. The THC would block the neuropathic pain that the patient was experiencing, and help stimulate appetite. While the CBD would reduce inflammation, help stimulate the immune system, and improve focus. As an added benefit of using an equal ratio of THC and CBD, the CBD suppresses the psychoactive properties of the THC. This means that the patient gets the benefits of the THC without feeling the psychoactive properties of the THC, including the "stoners high", paranoia, anxiety, and sedation.

Without getting into biochemistry, let me talk about how this ratio stimulates appetite. Basically, the ratio stimulates the part of the brain that regulates hunger, causing you to become hungry. So, obviously, with increased hunger comes increased appetite, and the person is more likely to eat more than they would when they're suffering from pain or not feeling well.

When we had our follow-up appointment one month later, the patient reported that the pain had been reduced, and their appetite had returned. Fast forward seven months, the patient entered the office with family members. My medical assistant informed me that the patient's family wanted to meet me. They were so elated and wanted to thank me. The patient was also excited, as they hadn't been able to work for a long time, and had been feeling dependent. When the patient asked me about returning to work, I smiled, and said, *"Absolutely!"*

With this case, I was able to nail the treatment protocol on the first try. Typically, when I meet with a patient, after I certify that they qualify for the use of Medical Marijuana, and we put together the health plan, I then see that patient a month later to assess their progress. Of course, at any time, the patient can email me with any questions or concerns. After the first month, I look at the treatment protocol and discuss with the patient what responses they are having, and assess if it is having the desired effect for the patient. If everything seems good, I then see the patient every four months to continually monitor their progress. It has been two years since our initial appointment. The patient continues to do well with the current protocol and I'm happy that I was able to help improve their quality of life.

The Simple Addition Of Medical Marijuana Did The Trick!

Chapter 3

Traumatic Brain Injury

This is an unfortunate case where the injury could have been avoided. The patient was involved in a high velocity impact car crash resulting from the other driver being under the influence of alcohol. During impact, the patient hit their head on the windshield which resulted in an acceleration-deceleration injury. What this means, in layman terms, is that the brain slams into the inside of the skull. This results in the stretching and tearing of nerve tissues called sheering axon injury. This leads to permanent neurological damage.

According to the United States Centers for Disease Control and Prevention (CDC), there are approximately 1.5 million people in the United States who suffer from a traumatic brain injury (TBI) each year. Of these cases, the CDC has estimated that 85,000 suffer long term disabilities as a result of these injuries. Many in the medical field believe these statistics are on the low side due to non-reporting and/or misdiagnosis.

Research shows that TBI is twice as likely to occur among men than women. This has been surmised to be as a result of men engaging more frequently in risky behavior. The most common activities that lead to TBI are car accidents, the use of firearms and falls.

The patient entered my office in a wheelchair and escorted by family members. I immediately noted a surgical scar on the scalp. The family filled out the paperwork as the patient was unable hold the pen and write clearly. Before I began the exam, it was explained to me the history regarding the injury.

My philosophy, when working with a patient is to Look, Listen and Feel, as stated earlier in this book, If a doctor is just prescribing to the symptoms, they are neither looking, listening or feeling their patient.

When I performed the patient's physical exam, the patient exhibited weakness in the upper and lower extremities with a mild tremor. The patient stated, *"My legs feel so heavy that I am unable to walk more than a few feet so I am stuck in this wheelchair."* Patient went on to explain that they live with constant headaches.

I knew right away that an equal ratio of THC - CBD would be the best bet for the patient. Almost in tears during the appointment, due to the chronic and intense pain, the patient was almost to the point of giving up. When I explained how Medical Marijuana could help, I could see the relief in their face. I explained how THC has neuropathic pain reduction properties that would help reduce their pain. I further explained how the CBD, which has anti-spasmatic properties, could possibly help decrease their tremors. The patient understood right away how this natural medicine might relieve the pain they had been experiencing for so long.

Essentially, my first goal, was to reduce the headache pain the patient was suffering from. In addition to pain reduction, I wanted to try and reduce the tremors to help improve their fine motor skills.

For daytime use, I prescribed an equal ratio of THC - CBD as this ratio has shown to work best to reduce tremors and pain. At night-time, I prescribed a High THC - Low CBD ratio as this ratio has shown to work best to reduce pain enabling the patient to get good night sleep. With this protocol, I was able to reduce the headache pain and tremors almost immediately. The proof that this was the proper regimen came during the one-month follow-up appointment. The patient was already reporting a reduction in pain and noticed that the tremors were slightly reduced. Two years later, the patient remains on the same protocol. They are still experiencing pain but the level of pain is now tolerable.

This Was A Difficult Case, As I Wish I Could Do More!

Chapter 4

Parkinson's Disease

A patient arrived on a rainy morning for their first appointment in my office. Upon first observation, the patient appeared alert but was showing extrapyrimidal symptoms; symptoms associated with an individual suffering from Parkinson's Disease. These symptoms included pill rolling tremors, the most common tremor associated with Parkinson's Disease and non-stop lip smacking.

Parkinson's Disease is a progressive nervous system disorder that affects movement. The symptoms are the result of the gradual degeneration of nerve cells in the portion of the midbrain that controls body movements. The first signs are likely to be barely noticeable; a feeling of weakness or stiffness in one limb, or a fine trembling of one hand when it is at rest. Eventually, the tremors worsen and spread, muscles become stiffer, movements slow down, and balance and coordination deteriorate. As the disease progresses, depression, cognitive issues, and other mental or emotional problems are commonly seen.

The patient was extremely anxious as they stated that they were unable to fill out the forms that my medical assistant had handed them. The patient stated, "I cannot use my hands. Look how much they shake." The patient was to the point of an emotional breakdown. I walked up to the patient, gave a hug and assured the patient not to worry that the paper work would be filled out. You could actually see the relief in their eyes that someone understood the situation and was willing to help in any, and all ways needed.

As I began my initial history and physical, the patient began telling me a story. They had been living with Parkinson's Disease for many years and the progression of the disease had resulted in the inability to meet with clients face to face. For reference, I'm sure many of you know the well-known actor, Michael J. Fox, and his very public struggle with Parkinson's Disease. Being an A-List celebrity, producers, writers and directors were more than willing to write roles that would incorporate his disease. This enabled him to continue working in show business and, also resulted in making the public aware of this terrible degenerative disease. Michael J Fox is the exception rather than the rule.

31

Most people suffering with Parkinson's do not have the luxury of having their professional environment willing to cater to the symptoms of their disease. As this patient stated, *"With my medical condition, I cannot hold face to face meetings anymore. Them seeing me like this would turn business away!"*

We discussed how the diagnosis of Parkinson's Disease was made since there was no known specific test in existence to actually diagnose the disease. The patient said they began experiencing some slight tremors and went to see a neurologist, who had been recommended to them by a close friend. The neurologist was able to diagnose Parkinson's Disease based upon the patient's medical history, a review of the signs and symptoms, and a neurological and physical examination. I inquired if the doctor had ordered any other lab tests, such as blood tests, to rule out other conditions that could also be causing the symptoms. Patient replied that indeed they had undergone additional testing to rule out other causes.

I then inquired if any medications were prescribed to help with the symptoms, as there is no cure for Parkinson's Disease. Medications are used to help manage problems with walking, movement and tremors. These medications increase or substitute for dopamine that is not being supplied naturally by the brain. People with Parkinson's Disease have low brain dopamine concentrations. However, dopamine can't be given directly, as it can't enter your brain. Patient stated they had tried these medications, and that they had lived with the side effects of them. Over time, the benefits of the medications had diminished and become less consistent.

Medications that may be prescribed to treat the symptoms include, but are not limited to:

Carbidopa-Levodopa: This is the most effective Parkinson's disease medication. It is a natural chemical that passes into your brain and is converted to dopamine. The side effects of this drug may include nausea, light-headedness and involuntary movements.

Dopamine Agonists: Unlike levodopa, dopamine agonists don't change into dopamine. Instead, they mimic dopamine effects in your brain. They aren't as effective as Levodopa in treating your symptoms, but they last longer. Side effects of dopamine agonists are similar to the side effects of carbidopa-levodopa, but they can also include hallucinations, sleepiness and compulsive behaviors.

MAO B Inhibitors: These medications help prevent the breakdown of brain dopamine by inhibiting the brain enzyme monoamine oxidase B (MAO B). Side effects may include nausea or insomnia. Often used in conjunction with Carbidopa-Levodopa, these medications increase the risk of hallucinations.

After reviewing the patient's history of their Parkinson's Disease, I then discussed with the patient the benefits that Medical Marijuana could provide. The plan I envisioned would reduce the extrapyrimidal symptoms the patient was experiencing and slow down the progression of the disease, as much as possible. I prescribed the patient Medical Marijuana with a Low THC -High CBD ratio, for daytime and a High THC - Low CBD ratio, for night-time. The High CBD, for use during the day, would help decrease the tremors and muscle spasms thus making movement easier. For night, the High THC would help reduce any associated pain, enabling the patient to get a good night's sleep.

At the one month follow up, the patient entered my office with a completely new outlook on life. As soon as the patient saw me, I was given a positive nod and a "*thumbs up*". With the use of Medical Marijuana, their symptoms had improved, and they were enjoying a better quality of life. After two years of treatment, the patient decided to retire so they could enjoy the rest of their life.

The Patient Is Quietly Enjoying Retirement.

Chapter 5

Diabetic Neuropathy

This patient is a great, gregarious person that I have enjoyed working with. When the patient first came into the office, despite the pain they said, *"Hey, how are you?!"* While the patient was bright, alert and mentally very sharp, they were, unfortunately, suffering from obesity and Type 2 diabetes. As a result, the patient was experiencing bilateral, lower extremity neuropathy. This is a fancy way to say that both lower extremities were in pain, due to diabetic-related nerve damage.

When someone first enters my office, I look for signs and symptoms above what the patient is relating to me. I am looking for any subtle neurological abnormalities. If you've ever wondered why a doctor asks you questions like, *"So, where are you today? What's today's date? What year is it?"* or asks you to follow their finger with your eyes, it's because the doctor is looking for subtle changes that might indicate neurological deficits.

The patient showed no signs of any impairment, mentally or emotionally. Throughout the initial appointment, we chatted freely, and even shared a laugh or two. The patient's primary complaint was chronic pain due to complications of their diabetes. As diabetes advances, the arteries start to clog, making them smaller and smaller, resulting in decreased blood flow to the extremities. The decreased blood flow leads to a lack of oxygen and nutrients to the peripheral limbs and nerve endings. Without the proper blood flow, the nerves do not perform at their optimal level.

There are two types of diabetes. Type 1 diabetes is a medical condition where the cells within the pancreas no longer produces insulin, and the patient must self-inject insulin in order to control their blood sugar levels. This often shows up in childhood, but it can also appear in adulthood.

Type 2 diabetes is a medical condition that is directly related to obesity. The more excess weight someone carries, the harder it is for insulin to bind with the receptors on the cells within the body. Thus, making it harder to drive sugar into the cell. This is called insulin resistance. Without the insulin binding to the cell, sugars are unable to fuel the cells to insure everything is working properly. It's like trying to fill up your gas tank, with the gas flowing OUTSIDE of the intake pipe - you'll get a little bit of gas in the tank, but not enough to operate your car efficiently.

As diabetes progresses, patients experience a variety of different symptoms. In terms of diabetic neuropathy, they experience two different distinct symptoms. First, they experience severe pain. This is similar to the pain you feel when you cross your legs or feet for an extended amount of time and cut off the blood flow. That feeling of pins and needles is very similar to what a person suffering with diabetic neuropathy feels, all the time, day in and day out.

As the diabetes progresses, the second symptom, a loss of sensation in the extremities will occur. As a result, the patient can no longer feel pain and therefore can cause damage to their extremities without them knowing it. For instance, they can cut their toes or feet, not feel it or notice it, and it can become infected sometimes to the point of requiring amputation. The good news is diabetes is very controllable, and, if the patient follows dietary guidelines, the progression of the disease can be slowed down.

When the patient first came to see me, they were experiencing the first symptom of diabetic neuropathy, severe pain. The pain was felt in both feet which affected the patient's ability to walk. My conversation with this patient was not just how to relieve the pain, but how to slow down the progression of their diabetes.

First, I educated the patient on how to regulate blood sugar levels through diet modification, exercise and weight reduction. Next, I explained the two different components of Medical Marijuana, THC and CBD, and how a combination of both can help reduce the symptoms. After considering all factors, I prescribed an equal ratio of THC - CBD, for daytime use, to help alleviate both the pain and inflammation. For night-time use, I prescribed a High THC – Low CBD ratio, to ensure the pain would not affect the sleep cycle. Sleep is an essential part of an individual's well-being.

Fortunately, my patient was a very compliant. The patient took their own health seriously and understood that by following the regimen I prescribed, they had the power to improve their own quality of life. When the patient first came in to see me, the patient was taking a narcotic pain killer. The patient said to me, *"Doc, I don't want to be on these narcotics, anymore. They're making me sick, and I'm still in pain. I'll do whatever it takes to get better."*

Heavy duty pain-killers, specifically those of narcotic strength, do often make people sick. Even if their pain is relieved, they often experience nausea, tiredness, and constipation.

So, what do conventional doctors do? They prescribe medication for "narcotic induced constipation." Maybe you've seen the ads on television for these types of products. Using one harmful drug to "fix" the side-effects of another harmful drug. This is what we are able to move away from when we treat the entire person, versus just throwing pills at the various symptoms.

For years, the patient had progressed classically through a variety of "pain killers." From acetaminophen to ibuprofen, to higher and higher doses of narcotics, with no relief and no resolution. Before starting a regimen which included the use of Medical Marijuana, the patient was basically taking opium, which is what oxycodone, methadone, and fentanyl all are.

After years of suffering, within a month, the patient told me, *"Doc, I'm feeling great. I can't believe it."* They walked into my office, without limping, smiling from ear to ear, and added, *"Well, I'm a lot better!"* Most of the symptoms had resolved, and the use of narcotic pain killers was greatly decreased. *"I've got my life back, Doc!"* I could hardly believe my eyes, the difference in just one month.

By the fourth month, the patient had completely stopped taking narcotics pain killers, had lost 55 pounds and had gotten their blood sugars under control. The patient told me once that walking with the diabetic neuropathy, was like trying to walk on hot coals. No longer, the patient now takes nice long walks and continues to work to achieve optimal health.

Be Proactive And Take Control Of Your health!

Chapter 6

Multiple Sclerosis

When this patient first came to my office, they had already received a diagnosis of Multiple Sclerosis (MS) eleven years prior and were exhibiting pain with associated muscle spasms in their upper extremities. The patient was an athlete, and had noticed, while on a strict detox diet, fatigue, and muscle weakness started to develop. They initially believed that this was due to the detox diet they were on and physical stress of training. As the symptoms progressed, the patient developed horizontal double vision. With the onset of this new symptom, the patient immediately made an appointment with a neurologist. The neurologist suspected MS and ordered an MRI diagnostic study which confirmed the diagnosis of MS. Unhappy with the options offered by the neurologist, the patient began researching alternative treatments for MS. They discovered that MS was one of the conditions approved by New York State to be treated with Medical Marijuana.

Typically, a MS patient will be prescribed an anti-inflammatory, a muscle relaxer and a pain killer. The medications are used in conjunction to reduce inflammation, minimize spasms and relieve pain. As the symptoms of the disease increase, the strength of the medications must be increased to compensate for the advancing symptoms. As a result, the patient often moves into heavy-duty narcotics to control the severe pain, spasms and cramps that can occur.

At the initial office visit, the patient stated, *"The symptoms I am experiencing have caused me to lose my career and my life seems to be going in a downward spiral!"*. Throughout the exam, the patient made it very clear that they were concerned about the career options that would be available to them as the disease progressed. **Who could blame them?** MS often progresses and causes debilitation and lack of mobility. At this time, no cure exists. Depression is not an uncommon as patients grapple with a loss of quality of life.

MS is a disease of the myelin sheath covering the nerves of the central nervous system. Myelin is comprised primarily of fats and proteins, and functions to protect the nerve endings. It also insulates neurons so they can send nerve signals quickly and efficiently. When a patient suffers from MS, the myelin sheath is breaking down, and nerves are left unprotected. This process is known as demyelination, and causes the nerve functions to slow down, or even stop.

Think of your central nervous system, for example, as a power cord. The wires in the cord conduct electricity, and the plastic covering over the cord protects the wires that conduct the electricity, and allow that electricity to flow freely and efficiently. The plastic covering also ensures that the flow of the electricity stays in a straight line, within the structure of the plastic covering. That's how the myelin sheath works in your body.

There are a few differences, of course. Surrounding the central nervous system, for instance, the myelin sheath has little gaps to help nerve signals move faster. With MS, the size of those gaps increase causing the nerve impulses to slow down, and the myelin sheath, overall, is weakened as well. When an MRI diagnostic test is performed, we are able to see the damage to the myelin sheath.

The cause of MS is not really known, although it appears as if genetics do play a role. It is considered an autoimmune disease, which is any condition where the body's immune system is attacking a part of the body.

With MS, the immune system is attacking the myelin sheath. During active "attack" stage, the disease is said to be in "relapse," and in quieter times, when the attacking stage is limited, it is called, "remission." These relapse/remission cycles can last hours, days, weeks, and even months.

Of the patients with these relapse/remission cycles, 60 - 70% eventually develop a constant or steady progression of the disease, with or without periods of remission. Some patients move into gradual and steady progression, with no periods of remission.

As the disease progresses, the gaps in the myelin sheath continue to increase, thus resulting in the nerve impulse slowing down and eventually stopping. It's almost as if you made multiple incisions in your power cord - one cut wouldn't stop electricity from flowing, but multiple cuts, or gaps, spaced throughout the cord, would certainly slow the flow, and maybe even cut-off electricity flow, completely.

As the gaps increase in the myelin sheath, the patient starts to exhibit symptoms. Different patients will exhibit different symptoms based upon the nerve fibers being affected within the central nervous system. This occurs as the flow of the nerve signal is disrupted. As the disease continues to progress, patients lose motor skill abilities, have balance problems, experience muscle spasms or uncontrollable muscle contractions, blurred vision, problems eating and sleeping, as well as other related difficulties.

I educated the patient on how Medical Marijuana might help. The primary goal was to decrease the inflammation in the myelin sheath, and in the body, reduce the muscle spasms, reduce pain and hopefully slow the progression of the disease. I prescribed a Low THC - High CDB ratio for day time use, and a High THC - Low CBD ratio for night-time, as the patient was experiencing terrible muscle spasms and cramping at night. The patient really needed to sleep in order to feel better.

A reduction in inflammation is key with this disease. The body has an innate ability to heal itself. What hampers healing is inflammation. So, if we can reduce excessive inflammation, the body has the ability to heal itself. Excessive inflammation occurs with poor nutrition, stress, disease conditions, and external stressors. CBD helps reduce inflammation in the body, so it becomes an important part of the healing process for patients who are experiencing symptoms or diseases related to excessive inflammation in the body.

CBD is not a silver bullet when it comes to inflammation. Everyone is different. How quickly it works in the body will depend on a person's overall health, metabolism rate, and length of inflammation or disease cycle. For some people, the anti-inflammatory action is very quick; within one or two doses. For others, it might take a few weeks, or even months.

At the one-month follow-up, the patient reported that they were feeling better, in general, and that the Medical Marijuana that I had prescribed had resulted in reduced pain and muscle spasms.

Medical Marijuana is different than narcotic pain killers. Since such small amounts of THC and CBD are being used, it is much more difficult, and would take much longer, to build up a tolerance to the medication as compared to narcotic pain killers. The addictive action of narcotic pain killers are well documented; for some individuals, just one to two pills creates a craving, and develops into a dependence or addiction. Narcotic painkillers are opioids being prescribed by physicians; one of the most highly addictive substances known to man. We are experiencing an epidemic in narcotic pain killer overdose deaths in this country, and I believe these deaths could be avoided if we looked at alternatives, like Medical Marijuana.

Research has shown that THC and CBD are not nearly as addictive as narcotic painkillers and there is little to no possibility of overdosing. Therefore, when the dosage has to be increased, there is not as much concern when using Medical Marijuana as compared to narcotic painkillers.

Every patient is different. For some, the disease barely progresses after diagnosis. Others move through a debilitating progression in a matter of a few years, becoming wheelchair bound and physically disabled relatively quickly. Some patients experience "flare-ups" where symptoms are much worse than at other times. No two patients experience MS the same way.

The goal of the physician is to help the patient increase their quality of life, slow the progression of the disease, and hopefully extend the patient's life. As an incurable disease, and one that does progress, it's typical that the patient will die eventually from complications due to MS. But even though the prognosis may seem bleak, it's important to help out, stay positive, and work together, with the patient, to increase quality and length of life.

Two and a half years later, I am happy to report that this patient is still narcotic pain killer free. They maintain their health through behavioral modification, that includes, an anti-inflammation diet and an exercise program as well as adhering to the Medical Marijuana regimen initially implemented.

Say Yes To Medical Marijuana!

Chapter 7

Breast Cancer and Related Pain

This patient entered my office, clearly in pain. Slightly hunched over, with very slow movements, they were walking as if they were someone many years older. This always breaks my heart when I see patients in this kind of pain, and I can't imagine living with something like this, chronically, as this patient had for months.

At the time of the first visit, the patient had been diagnosed with breast cancer, and was already under the care of an oncologist and surgical oncologist. Even though the patient was taking pain medications, they didn't work through the deep pain that the patient was experiencing; the main complaint was the pain that could be seen written all over the patient's face, so it was clear where we needed to start.

What typically happens when a patient is in pain, is that their physician will initially recommend over the counter pain medications such as Advil, Tylenol or Aleve. If this works in reducing the pain for the patient, then the physician doesn't need to advance the strength of the medication. However, if the pain is not reduced, then the physician will increase the strength of the over-the-counter medication. If the pain fails to subside, the physician will advance to a prescribed pain killer such as Tylenol 3 or Tylenol 4.

The final step, if the pain persists, would be for a physician to prescribe a narcotic pain killer such as Oxycodone or Fentanyl, or one of the many other narcotic drugs. It's the physician's responsibility to start a patient on the lowest dose needed to reduce the pain and to advance the class of pain killer only as needed.

This patient had gone through the entire buffet of pain medications out there, to the point now that they were wearing a slow-release fentanyl transdermal patch. Fentanyl is one of the strongest pain killers available. It's a narcotic pain killer, which means it's highly addictive and possible side effects include dizziness, constipation, anxiety and hallucinations.

It's not unusual for patients to develop an addiction to the fentanyl patch; they start craving the pain relief provided by the fentanyl, while their body develops a tolerance to the drug. Patients apply more and more patches to achieve the same level of relief, and can overdose inadvertently.

At that initial visit, the patient explained to me that the primary goal was to wean off of the fentanyl patch but still experience pain relief. When I discussed Medical Marijuana and the benefits of its use, I explained that, not only could it provide pain relief, but, also, possibly, slow the spread of cancerous cells, in the body.

The patient was certainly, and understandably, open to starting the Medical Marijuana treatment especially after having an aggressive invasive surgical procedure; this included a mastectomy, which is the removal of the mammary glands and related lymph nodes, and part of the pectoral muscle. This aggressive procedure resulted in scar tissue formation and muscle tightness, both of which caused extreme chest and ribcage pain.

The patient saw the potential of Medical Marijuana as a blessing; in addition to weaning off the synthetic pain killers, it could possibly help to decrease the cancer in the body. The patient looked at me, through strained, tired eyes, and said, *"I just want to get off of this stuff. I want to feel like myself again, But, without them, my pain is completely unmanageable."*

I see it over and over again in my office. Patients come in suffering from severe pain, and basically addicted to narcotic pain killers. These pain killers control the patient, versus helping the patient control their pain and improve their quality of life. While on narcotic pain killers, the brain chemistry is altered in order to decrease the pain, but, the adverse reaction to the medication is that core personalities traits start to change.

Sometimes people around the patient don't recognize the person that the patient has become while on narcotic pain killers (more on this in a few chapters). This is no way to live, and I celebrate any person who enters my office with the goal of weaning off narcotic pain killers. So, the patient and I forged on, looking to see how we could achieve the desired health goals.

I said to the patient, *"Give me some time, and hopefully we can get you off the patch."*

I started off with an equal ratio of THC - CBD during the day time, with a High THC - Low CBD ratio for the night-time, to help the patient sleep and get some much needed rest. Both THC and CBD have shown promise in slowing the growth of cancer cells, and even possibly having cancer cell killing capabilities. This is new research, so we will know more in a few years, but, for now, I work with the emerging science to help my patients.

This patient was wearing the fentanyl patch, which basically meant that the body was absorbing fentanyl twenty-four hours a day, seven days a week. Each patch lasts up to 72 hours, and during the time that the patch is worn, the drug is constantly being released into the body, via the skin.

Anytime you are dealing with a patient who has a dependence on a narcotic pain killer, you must move slowly.

If you go too quickly, the patient can unnecessarily suffer through severe withdrawal symptoms. To avoid this, I institute a slow tapering off of the narcotic pain killer, while introducing non-addictive pain relief, Medical Marijuana, into the patient's regimen.

Keep in mind, a drug dependency or addiction isn't just physical. When you have an addiction or dependence on a drug, you also have a psychological addiction, which is sometimes more difficult to triumph over. The psychological aspect of the addiction is the understandably desirable feeling of experiencing less pain, and sometimes even the "high" feeling. You're not in pain anymore, or not in as much pain, and that feels good. So, even if a physical addiction hasn't developed, that psychological stronghold can be very difficult to release.

Some people have a propensity to addiction; whether that addiction is sugar, gambling, or sex - it doesn't matter. These people take things to an extreme, and have a hard time saying "no" and stopping destructive behavior. Individuals who do not have an addictive personality find it easier to stop destructive behaviors. So, sometimes it's the psychological dependency that sustains the addiction, over what's happening in the brain and body.

When this is the case, sometimes you have to work with the patient to change their behavior so that they don't have the same psychological triggers that got them into the situation they are in. I will coach them on changing their behavior, changing the people that they are around, and changing out destructive things in their life. This can literally mean walking down different streets to avoid making contact with certain dealers of street "drugs." In other words, you can't treat the addiction, without helping the person behind the addiction.

Memory cells in the brain are easily influenced. If you trigger a memory cell with a negative behavior, like drug addiction, that mental/psychological memory will trigger the person to engage in the harmful behavior again. We don't want to stimulate the memory cells that crave the drugs that we're trying to break free from.

There are medications that can be prescribed to help someone who is heavily addicted to certain drugs and medications. They can reduce withdrawal symptoms, anxiety and other side effects like increased heart rate, sweating, etc. So, again, a holistic approach can really be helpful.

Fortunately, this patient had a very strong personality and was ready to take on the challenge of weaning off the narcotic pain killer. Through strength and perseverance, they were able to reduce their fentanyl dose to the point that they were completely weaned off of it.

Depending on the person, weaning off of a narcotic pain killer can take a few weeks, or several months. If the person is on a strong dose, and has been for several years, it will take longer to wean them off. On the other hand, if the person has only been on the narcotic pain killer for a short period of time, and isn't susceptible to psychological addiction, this process can take less time.

As a person is weaning off the narcotic pain killer, it is important to control any withdrawal symptoms. If the patient experiences any withdrawal symptoms, the patient will feel very sick, and will have the urge to resume use of the narcotic pain killer to avoid the discomfort they feel. By weaning a patient slowly, the brain can be tricked into thinking it still has the drug that it's addicted to but, in reality, it is being substituted with a non-narcotic pain killer.

The patient and I worked together closely. At the one month follow up, the patient was happy with the results, and was especially appreciative of the High THC - Low CBD ratio that I had prescribed. I eventually decided on a High THC - Low CBD ratio of 6:1 during the daytime, and a High THC - Low CBD ratio of 20:1 for the evening. The patient always had a positive, strong mindset since I first met them at my office. The transformation to living with manageable pain, and completely weaning off fentanyl, resulted in a much higher quality of life. While not pain free, the patient feels that finally their life is under their control. The patient is right where they want to be- fentanyl free!

Just Say No To Narcotics!

Chapter 8

Severe Back Pain - Refused Surgery

This patient came into my office complaining of severe back pain. Upon observation, I noticed the patient walking with a single leg cane and wearing a lumbar support. They explained that approximately 10 years earlier, they were involved in a motor vehicle accident resulting in a herniated disc and was diagnosed with lumbar radiculopathy.

Very often, patients come into my office having experienced some sort of trauma to their body, which results in tissue damage leading to chronic pain. In some cases, someone, who has been hurt in an automobile accident or at work, may sustain an injury of the lumbar spine but the body is able to heal itself within a few weeks. However, there are cases where the back injury can be more serious. These injuries can result in a bulging disc or a disc herniation. This damaged disc(s) can then pinch a nerve(s), which oftentimes results in severe pain, that can become chronic or long-lasting. Often the pain will radiate down into their upper extremities, depending on the severity of the injury. This type of pain is known as radiculopathy.

To picture what a herniated disc looks like, imagine a jelly-filled donut; one that's super fresh, with pretty white powder on it. Think of that as the disc. If the disc, or donut, gets pressed down a little, a small amount of jelly would ooze out of that donut. That would resemble what a disc bulge is like. When you see a donut that is smushed down so much that all the jelly is almost out, that would resemble a disc herniation.

The structure of spinal discs changes so much, when an injury like this occurs, that the function of the disc deteriorates. The change in disc shape causes the disc to push on the nerve, thus pinching it. As you can imagine, this becomes quite painful. It causes the pain to radiate into the extremities. How and when it hurts can vary depending on the individual. Sometimes the pain can lessens with gentle movement; but, at other times, it can get worse with movement. Simple life functions, such as sitting, walking, lying down or standing, can become extremely difficult and painful.

The inflammation cycle can be devastating, causing further injury and pain. Let's take a closer look with the example of our herniated disc, like this patient was suffering from. The herniated disc started to impinge on the nerve, which caused an irritation and inflammation of the nerve root. The surrounding and supporting tissue of the nearby muscles are affected as well with irritation and inflammation resulting in discomfort.

During the history and physical, the patient complained of severe neck pain that is progressively getting worse. They were prescribed narcotic pain killers by their primary doctor, but they provided little long-term relief. After exhausting conservative care, they were referred to an Orthopedic Surgeon. After an examination, the surgeon recommended surgery. Surgery is often recommended to either remove a portion of the disc that's herniated, or to completely remove the disc and fuse the two segments of the spine together.

"Doc, I just don't want that surgery. I think it will make it worse," the patient exclaimed to me. *"But, I just can't handle this pain. Is there any way you can help me avoid getting cut open?"*

I agreed with the patient that surgery should be a last resort. As our founding father of medicine, Hippocrates, stated, *"Natural forces within us are the true healers of disease."* Surgery may be recommended but there is no guarantee that it is going to be successful. There are times

56

when surgery is unnecessary, and can actually do further damage. Conversely, there is absolutely a time and place for surgery but, if it's not a life-threatening situation, and the patient wants to explore other options, I support and respect a patient's decision to do so.

With today's cutting edge medical technology, if a patient does elect to have a surgical procedure, this procedure can be performed with minimal invasiveness and less strain on the body. Laser and laparoscopic techniques continue to improve, and offer a safer alternative for patients who really do need surgical intervention.

Having made the decision not to have surgery, the patient wanted my help. They asked,

"Can you help reduce the pain? Even just enough so that I feel like myself, again. Right now I can hardly stand it."

The patient had been prescribed narcotic pain killers but was very uncomfortable with the idea of taking them long term. They feared that they would become dependent on them, and have to take them for the rest of their life to keep their pain levels tolerable.

I discussed with the patient what other options were available and how these options could help manage the pain. I explained how using the proper ratio of THC - CBD would be able to reduce her pain and inflammation. I recommended an equal THC - CBD ratio, for day time use. That ratio would provide adequate inflammatory and pain reduction. I explained, this ratio has an added benefit. When CBD equals THC, CBD suppresses the THC's psychoactive properties without reducing its pain reduction properties. *"I think this will give you some comfort, so you can enjoy your day."* I told the patient.

For night-time, I recommended a High THC - Low CBD ratio. This ratio provides the greatest amount of pain relief enabling a better night's sleep. As I've talked about earlier, but it bears repeating, sleep is an essential aspect of the healing process. A person simply cannot function if they aren't getting enough quality sleep and their circadian rhythm is out of sync. Circadian rhythm is our internal clock. The natural clock for humans is that we sleep at night, and we are awake during the day. Nocturnal animals have a different clock or cycle, and are active during the night, and are asleep during the day. The High THC sedation properties help improve sleep - wake cycle.

Since the patient was taking narcotic pain killers, and had been for some time, I had to carefully taper the patient off the narcotic pain killers. I do this to avoid withdrawal symptoms, while not losing the pain relief benefits that the patient was experiencing. I don't want my patients to become uncomfortable during this weaning off process. So, as I slowly decrease the level of narcotic pain killer use, I increased the use of the Medical Marijuana to make up for the needed pain relief.

I do this slowly, so that I can find what I call the "sweet spot," where the patient is using just the right amount of Medical Marijuana. What determines the "sweet spot" ? It is unique for each patient. Factors such as: a patient's personality, their amount of pain and tolerance for that pain, their metabolism level, as well as many other factors play a part in this determination. Every patient is different, so it takes time to find the proper amount of Medical Marijuana that will work for each person.

The patient is doing great on the prescribed regimen of Medical Marijuana. After only one month of treatment with Medical Marijuana, the pain became tolerable, and after a year the patient was able to discontinue use of all narcotic pain killers. The patient is enjoying life again and living life to the fullest.

I believe that as the acceptance and use of Medical Marijuana increase for chronic pain and inflammation relief, there will be a decrease in the number of narcotic related overdoses. At least, this is my hope, and one of the main reasons that I'm so passionate about the use of Medical Marijuana.

Medical Marijuana: A Natural Supplement!

Chapter 9

Irritable Bowel Disease: Crohn's

When this patient first entered my office, I saw a fit, but underweight, young individual who should have been experiencing the prime of life. At the age of 10, the patient was diagnosed with Crohn's disease by a GI doctor. At the time of the patient's first visit, while taking a history and physical, the patient shook their head and said, *"Doc, my condition is making my social life very difficult. I'm like those commercials - I'm always looking for where the nearest restroom is when I'm out and about."* Then added, *nervously,* *"Forget about going on a date."* As a very family oriented, spiritual, young individual, the patient was hoping to marry one day, have kids, and raise a family. But, the Crohn's was ruining that.

"I don't feel like I can go out and meet the right person with this condition. It's ruining my life."

Crohn's disease is different than ulcerative colitis. Both are inflammatory conditions of the GI tract, but ulcerative colitis is typically found in the colon, or large intestine. The inflammation that occurs with Crohn's can affect any part of the GI tract, from your mouth to the anus.

A lot of people confuse Irritable Bowel Syndrome (IBS) with Irritable Bowel Disease (IBD), but there's a very clear difference between the two. With IBS, what's affected are the muscle movements needed in order for the digestive tract to function normally; while IBD is an inflammatory condition. Crohn's Disease falls into the IBD category.

The cause of Crohn's is not fully understood, but the consensus is that it is an autoimmune disease. An autoimmune disease is a condition where the immune system attacks an organ or tissue in the body.

Some of the symptoms of Crohn's include; abdominal cramping, bloating, constipation or severe diarrhea, associated weight loss, and fatigue due to anemia. Some people are lucky enough to be symptom-free most of their lives, but other can have severe and chronic symptoms that never go away. At its worst, Crohn's disease can cause life-threatening complications, as the lining of the intestine may become compromised.

The chronic inflammation associated with Crohn's can sometimes cause scar tissue within the GI tract, weakening it, and causing permanent damage. Left untreated, an individual with Crohn's can become seriously ill due to; bowel obstructions, malnutrition, fistulas (openings into other body parts, like the bladder or uterus), colon cancer, and destructive forms of arthritis due to untreated inflammation in the body.

Crohn's patients are usually prescribed medications to reduce the spasms in the colon, and reduce inflammation. These medications include steroidal and non-steroidal anti-inflammatory drugs. If the symptoms become severe, the patient will be prescribed narcotic pain killers. If a patient has a severe episode, drugs that suppress the immune system can be prescribed. The main problem with immunosuppressive drugs is just that - they suppress the immune system. This can leave the patient vulnerable to other illnesses and infections, including an increased risk of cancer.

This patient was experiencing bloating, numerous, painful episodes of cramping, diarrhea, and general malaise (or just not feeling well). During the physical exam, I examined the stomach and noticed bloating in all four quadrants of the abdomen. Immediately after the exam, the patient had to leave the examination room to use the bathroom. *"See, Doc? This is what I'm talking about,"* the patient said as they exited the room.

As Crohn's disease is an inflammatory condition, the key is to calm the GI tract down by reducing the inflammation. Upon discussing the option of Medical Marijuana with the patient, I explained that CBD has anti-inflammatory properties that could help with the inflammation, thus reducing his symptoms. I recommended a Low THC - High CBD ratio for the daytime. For night-time, I recommended High THC - Low CBD ratio, for improved quality of sleep. In addition, I was hoping that the high THC would reduce the morning cramping pain that was being experienced.

After about a month, the patient came back for the first follow up appointment, and I immediately noticed that the patient had better color and their eyes were brighter. Excitedly, the patient told me, *" I feel so much better! My stools are more formed and, I am experiencing less constipation and diarrhea."* After hearing this, I suggested remaining on the Medical Marijuana regimen I had initially prescribed.

A year later, I almost didn't recognize the patient when they showed up for a one-year follow-up and re-certification. The patient had gained weight and looked healthy, versus the gaunt-like appearance I observed at the initial visit. I examined the patient's abdomen which didn't indicate any bloating and the patient didn't have to go to the bathroom right afterwards. The patient stated, *"Oh my gosh, Doc, I feel SO much better. Thank you!"*

Two years after the initial visit, the patient continues to improve, and now leads an active social life. During their visit the patient said, *"Doc, I want to tell you something."* I said, *"Uh oh, what's wrong?"*, *"Nothing, nothing! I met someone special. I just got engaged and we are planning the wedding."*

I see patients like this every day, and I realize how grateful I am to be able to help them. The effectiveness of Medical Marijuana is life-altering for these people. Those who had almost given up on ever having a complete life are now walking around free from narcotics, free from pain, and the stresses it causes on them and their loved ones.

I Love Making A Difference!

Chapter 10

Chronic Back Pain with Polysubstance Use

Before I even met this individual, I knew the patient was in trouble. The patient's significant other had called the office, crying, saying that the patient had been living for years with chronic severe pain. It was explained to me that they had seen many specialists, and didn't know what else to do. The patient was still in so much pain, and nothing seemed to be helping. The patient wanted to try something different. *"Do you think this might work?"* was asked of me referring to Medical Marijuana. *"Absolutely,"* I replied back, *"It won't hurt to try, and we'll give it our best shot."*

The patient's back pain wasn't psychosomatic. As I reviewed the patient's medical records, I noted the diagnosis for chronic lower back pain, with associated lumbar radiculopathy. This means the pain originates in the lower back and then travels down into the lower extremities. This type of pain can be very debilitating, leading to other issues, including mental health conditions such as anxiety and depression.

The MRI diagnostic study revealed which nerve was being compressed in the lumbar spine. An additional test, called the nerve conduction test, was performed which demonstrated nerve impulses were restricted by the injury. These two diagnostic studies confirmed the diagnosis of lumbar radiculopathy. This was a serious case, and the injury was significant.

During the history and physical, the patient's significant other did all of the speaking. I was told that the amount of medication taken changed the patient's personality and demeanor. The significant other said, "I've lost my partner!"

As I was sitting with the two of them, listening to their story, reading through the medical records, and looking at the laundry list of pain medications that were tried, and were currently being taken, I noticed that the patient hardly moved. The patient just sat there, still and silent. They were not looking around or showing any signs of interest. The patient just stared at the floor the entire time. The patient appeared to be in a drug-induced stupor.

During the physical exam, the patient made minimal eye contact with me, and reaction time to my questions, was delayed. The patient's mouth barely opened when responding with soft and slurred words. When I conducted active and passive range-of-motion testing (measuring how far the patient's limbs and joints could move), the patient indicated pain in the areas noted on the diagnostic studies.

The pain response wasn't the biggest concern to me. I was much more concerned about the possibility of being overmedicated. This was an individual who was clearly drugged-up on narcotic pain killers. What I noticed the most was how this young person, in what should be the prime of their life, was so far gone. The patient just wasn't there. The patient wasn't sharp, mentally or emotionally, and exhibited significant cognitive changes. In other words, the patient just couldn't think and process things normally. As a result of taking the narcotic pain killers, the patient developed anxiety and depression and, therefore, was also under the care of a psychiatrist.

Any time the pain medication was increased by the Physiatrist, the patient would exhibit behavioral side-effects. The Psychiatrist would then raise the dose of the behavioral medications that were prescribed to counter the side-effects produced by the narcotic pain killers. When the Psychiatrist changed the dosage, it would reduce the effectiveness of the pain medication. *"So, guess what would happen next?"* The strength of the narcotic pain killer would be increased. This became a vicious cycle resulting in the state of the patient that was sitting before me.

Since there was no communication between the Physiatrist and the Psychiatrist, drugs were being prescribed but no one was paying attention to how the drugs were affecting the patient. The patient was slowly being drugged to death. After reviewing the patient's medical records and listening to the history, I felt Medical Marijuana would be able to help. It would take some time, as I had to very slowly wean the patient off the narcotic pain killers, plus I had to deal with the behavioral medications.

Every medication has what is called a "therapeutic window". A therapeutic window is the range of doses that can be given to a patient to provide therapeutic relief without causing any significant adverse effects. Some medications have a small therapeutic window; while others are very large.

For medications that have a small therapeutic window, the prescriber must monitor the patient closely and carefully to ensure the patient is not being driven into a toxic range. If a patient is pushed into the toxic range, its means the patient is experiencing unwanted side-effects that could cause permanent harm, and even death. At this point, the risks of the drug outweigh the benefits of the drug.

My assessment was that the patient was either in the "toxic" range, or very close to it. The patient was shutting down both mentally and physically due to the side-effects from the excessive narcotic pain killers and behavioral medications. The fear that death could happen was a very real possibility. The significant other's concerns were not overblown. Coming into my office and trying to the wean the patient off the medications, by using Medical Marijuana, could very well save the patient's life.

My plan was to reduce the narcotic pain killers very slowly and, hopefully, reduce the severity of the psychological symptoms. I had to move cautiously as there are severe withdrawal symptom related to narcotic drug reduction, as well as with the reduction of behavioral medications. I almost felt as if the patient was abusing drugs, but only because the doctors were abusing their power to prescribe them and were not communicating with each other about the side effects.

Based on everything I needed to accomplish, with the use of Medical Marijuana, I prescribed an equal ratio of THC-CBD for the daytime, and a High THC - Low CBD ratio for the night-time. I wanted to make sure the patient experienced pain relief overnight and was able to get a good night sleep.

It's not uncommon for me to meet patients who are also taking anti-anxiety or antidepressant medications to combat the mental stress that comes from being in chronic pain. What I've found is that CBD helps keep someone emotionally balanced as it has anti-anxiety properties. So, sometimes we can taper off some of the behavioral medications because they're feeling better about themselves. They're more alert, and they're less anxious. When people start to feel better about themselves, things become "lighter", with less perceived burden and psychological stress. In addition to feeling better, this patient now would be less prone to injury.

CBD doesn't work in all cases. There are some patients who need to continue behavioral medications because of their condition; for example, if someone is suffering with schizophrenia, CBD may help keep them more balanced, but it won't replace the properties of the behavioral medications that are prescribed to reduce the hallucinatory symptoms of this debilitating mental health condition. It's important to remember that there are no magic bullets to take. Each patient needs to be evaluated to learn what will help, and what kind of health regimen will allow them to live their lives to the fullest.

They left the office, nervously. I could see that the significant other was truly concerned about the patient and was grieving a type of death, where physically the patient was there but not mentally and emotionally. The patient shuffled out of the office, still in a stupor, eyes glazed and mouth closed. I took a deep breath, and wished them well, hoping that we would see some improvement when they returned for the one month follow-up appointment.

Over the next month, as I was treating other patients, I kept thinking about this specific patient. I had a few conversations by phone and email, with the significant other, and I knew, at a minimum, things were not getting worse. The Medical Marijuana was having no negative effects on the patient. But I had underlying concerns about the patient weaning off of the narcotic pain killers and the behavioral medications.

Opioid-related deaths are at an all-time high in this country. In part, it is due to cases similar to this patient, where doctors prescribe narcotic pain killers. Sometimes, the doctor will observe what is happening to the patient and stop prescribing them. However, the patient, still in chronic severe pain, will simply go to another doctor, then another, and then another.

When the patient can no longer find a doctor willing to prescribe narcotic pain killers, the patient will hit the streets and will look for a local drug dealer to purchase narcotic pain killers. This puts the patient in a very dangerous position; not only because their addiction is out of control, but also because the quality of street drugs is certainly not guaranteed.

We've lost dozens of artists and celebrities who, sadly, put a face on this epidemic. Prince. Tom Petty. Philip Seymour Hoffman. Heath Ledger. Elvis. Even one of the fathers of psychology, Sigmund Freud, died of a morphine overdose.

Pictures of faces we all know doesn't really bring the horror of this epidemic home. In 2017, more than 72,000 Americans died due to drug overdoses, in this category of drugs. The sharpest increase was in overdoses related to synthetic opioids which jumped from around 2,500 deaths in 2013, to almost 30,000 in 2017. Take a look at those two numbers, again. From 2,500 to 30,000, in four years (these statistics are from the National Center for Health Statistics at the Centers for Disease Control (CDC). The CDC also has a searchable database, called CDC Wonder).

The opioid crisis in this country has progressed to the point that police officers, paramedics, and fire fighters all carry naloxone, a medication used to block the effects of narcotics, and to revive addicts who have overdosed. The other day, I saw a billboard encouraging family members and friends to get their hands on naloxone, to save the lives of their loved ones, if they are found overdosing.

What does it say about our country that our best "defense" against overdosing is a drug that revives addicts after they've overdosed? Naloxone saves lives, absolutely, and I do think that in this day and age, we should have it available to anyone who is living with or around someone who is addicted to opioids. But what if the message was, instead, to use non-addictive, effective pain killers like Medical Marijuana. *"How many lives could that save?"*

Some physicians believe in the use of THC and CBD to help their patients, and I do get some referrals from other doctors. There is a local psychiatrist, for example, who refers select clients to me for help with natural relief of their symptoms. Some doctors, however, are very resistant to the use of Medical Marijuana, and this is sometimes due to their training, or lack thereof. With that being said, there are some patients where it would be dangerous to wean them off some of their medications. Communication between doctors is critical. If we are to try and reduce the statistics of overdose deaths, doctors must start talking to each other.

I was concerned that my patient would become a statistic if I couldn't help. All I hoped was that the patient, with the significant other's help, would follow the regimen, and get out of danger. At the same time, the patient had recognized and documented lower back injuries that had to be addressed. The patient's cycle of pain needed to improve, or the patient would always be vulnerable.

At the one month follow-up, the patient definitely showed some improvement. It was minor, **but I'll take it.** The important thing was that the patient was slowly reducing the dosage of the narcotic pain killers, as well as the behavioral medications. I was hopeful, and kept my fingers crossed for the next visit, which would be at the four-month mark from our first appointment.

Three months later, as I was going through my calendar of patients, I saw that this patient was on the list. I was anxious for this patient to arrive, hoping that I would see an improvement immediately. When the patient walked into the office, I realized that I was meeting the patient for the very first time. This was no longer a drugged-out individual, shuffling through life in a drug induced stupor. The significant other was smiling, the patient was alert, made eye contact, and was very responsive to my questions. This was great news, and a great start.

At his eighth month follow-up, it was amazing to see the change in this individual. The significant other beamed and gave me a hug. *"I have my partner back!"* Not only was the patient free from narcotic pain killers, but had also weaned off all behavioral medications. The patient exclaimed *"I'm never taking that stuff again!"*

From that first meeting to the eight-month follow up, it was like I met two different people. At that first meeting, the patient could hardly walk, or lift their head. The patient was basically sleep-walking through life. When the patient walked into my office for that eight-month appointment, the patient strolled in quickly, smiled, said loudly, *"Hey doc! How are you doing?!"*

This Is Why I Do What I Do!

74

Chapter 11

Post Traumatic Stress Disorder

A patient came into the office after being diagnosed with severe anxiety and PTSD as a result of serving several tours of duty in war-ravaged countries. The patient had joined the military right out of high school. While serving, the patient was trained to do one job and one job only. Upon returning home after serving, they felt lost and afraid. I'll never forget the story shared with me about the difficult transition from military to civilian life, *"I'm lost, doc... I'm lost...."* the patient said, tears welling up, *"I was trained to do things that people don't understand. What am I going to do now?"*

At this point, the patient was having a hard time holding back tears. I stood up, and told the patient I understood, and gave the patient a hug. *"Everything's going to fine,"* I said,

"You're a United States soldier. The best there is... You're going to be fine. I'm here for you."

I escorted the patient into the back room of my office where I display my Civil War artifacts, along with my framed battle dress uniform and medals. I showed the patient the pictures of my family members, including Irish ancestors, who fought in the Civil War. I explained that, as a retired member and Commander of the New York Guard, 88th Brigade, 102 Forward Medical Support Detachment here in New York City, my primary responsibility was to maintain the wellness of and personal growth among my troops, as well as provide medical care to their families. I hoped by sharing my stories, the patient would understand that they were not alone.

We chatted, and talked, and chatted some more. I felt the patient relax, and we walked back into the consultation room to talk options. I told the patient, *"You have to take the same energy, and the same motivation of your training and now apply it to your civilian life."* But, how do you ask a soldier, who's only job in the Military was to kill our enemy, to now transition to civilian life?

With my military background, I tried to explain to the patient how this transition could look. *"This is what we can do, and this is how you can transition into a productive and fulfilling civilian life."* So much of my time and treatment of this patient was in the coaching realm. *"You were trained not to be reckless. You were trained to do certain things. This is* how you have to balance your life. Before you can do certain things, you have to make sure your life is balanced." Of course, I didn't experience exactly what my patient had experienced. So, I couldn't say "I know exactly how you feel." I think that would have minimized the patient's experience and lessened the impact of what was being dealt with. I did feel that, along with what I had experienced, plus my work with other veterans, I knew enough to know that the patient needed much more than a prescription for Medical Marijuana. The patient needed a life coach, and I was up to the task.

The patient and I spoke about how important it is to maintain physical health and grow mental and emotional muscles. I told him of my family's motto that had, ironically, come from a fortune cookie. "Inch by inch, life's a cinch; yard by yard, life is hard." Life can sometimes get very intense, but if we take things a step at a time, we can keep pushing through and overcome both physical and emotional obstacles.

Think about how, during missions, you're always checking in with your command center. "Are we cleared?," "No, you're not cleared." Are we cleared?," "No, you're not cleared." "Are we cleared?," "Yes, you're cleared." That's how you can get through this. Step by step. Making sure things are safe. I told the patient, "You can do this!"

The patient wasn't in pain, at least not physically, so I didn't have to focus on that aspect of care. Instead, we talked about how to focus energy and balance the emotional factors of everyday life. I also discussed how to reduce and manage the external stresses of everyday life by teaching different coping strategies.

For this patient, I needed a holistic approach, where the emphasis is placed on helping the patient heal, emotionally and spiritually. The first step was to choose the appropriate ratio of Medical Marijuana to help reduce the anxiety associated with the PTSD that the patient was suffering from. I prescribed a Low THC - High CBD ratio for daytime use, as this would keep the patient balanced and focused. CBD is great for this type of patient as it tends to "tone down" the anxiety associated with PTSD. As with all patients, a good night's sleep is essential for both physical and emotional stability. The patient was experiencing a hard time sleeping , especially when awoken by a stress episode. So, I prescribed a High THC - Low CBD ratio for the night-time.

Next, I suggested that the patient could benefit by enrolling in a post-active-duty support group. We're fortunate enough to have access to programs such as these, and I highly recommend this avenue for any military personnel suffering from PTSD. Many of these groups are run and managed by military wives whose husbands are either away on active duty, or who have lost their husbands in the line of duty.

At the first month follow-up visit, the patient was feeling better. Dealing with everyday civilian life was becoming a little easier each day. **This was encouraging to me**. For many soldiers, who return from active duty suffering from PTSD, it can take years, and sometimes decades, to feel better and be able to shake some of the tragic effects of PTSD. Sometimes, without proper treatment, the symptoms never disappear. This is evident by the high rate of suicides among veterans suffering with PTSD. It has been estimated that each day, 20 veterans suffering with PTSD, commit suicide. On average, male veterans are 18 times more likely to commit suicide than their civilian counterparts. Female veterans, on average, are 250 times more likely to commit suicide than their civilian counterparts. Unfortunately, in our country, veterans are not getting the help they so dearly need and deserve. **This needs to be changed!!**

HooooAH!

Chapter 12

Gastroparesis and Fibromyalgia

When this patient first came to the office, they were suffering and in a lot of pain. Whenever food was consumed, not only would they feel full very fast, a classic symptom of gastroparesis, but extreme nausea would follow. What was being consumed was irrelevant, it could be pepperoni pizza or plain white rice, but the results were the same. After almost each and every meal, the patient would experience nausea leading to vomiting. As you can imagine, the patient was unable to be involved in any social activities that included food. They were always hungry as the condition caused them to basically starve themselves. There was no motivation to eat. In addition to the nausea and vomiting, other symptoms included diarrhea, constipation, and acid reflux. Due to these symptoms, the patient was unable to maintain a healthy weight.

Additionally, the patient was experiencing severe pain of fibromyalgia, a nerve disorder affecting how the brain processes pain signals. Those suffering from fibromyalgia often experience widespread intense muscle pain and tenderness. These symptoms affect every day activities and take a toll on a person's social and professional life. This patient, like all my patients, had seen several physicians, including a gastroenterologist, a doctor who specializes in gastrointestinal (GI) disorders, who treated the patient's condition as per the usual protocol. Typically, this treatment includes non-narcotic pain relievers, medications that stimulate the stomach muscles, anti-nausea pills, and often, antidepressants. The patient had come to me, saying, *"You're my last resort,"* as their feeling was that they had exhausted all conventional western medicine.

The typical regimen gets complicated as medications used to calm spasms in the GI tract also result in the suppression of stimulation of other muscles within the whole body. Using these medications for calming spasm of the GI tract can result in constipation. Now, you need something to stimulate bowel movements, which sometimes hurts, as you can imagine.

Here's what makes it worse, I think. Very often, if you have a serious condition like this, you are under the care of several doctors. Those doctors rarely communicate with each other, so they may prescribe medications that counteract the effects of the other medications being prescribed. Doses often get raised, and the side-effects of the medications make the condition ultimately worse. This lack of continuity of care can make the patient even sicker; the doctors are treating the symptoms, and not the patient.

My philosophy, when working with a patient, is to Look, Listen and Feel, as stated earlier in this book. If a doctor is just prescribing to the symptoms, they are neither looking, listening or feeling their patient.

When I performed the patient's physical exam, everything "looked" normal, except when I examined the abdomen. It appeared and felt a little bit bloated, and the patient indicated some tenderness, which is common with gastroparesis. As I discussed the best course of treatment for the condition and symptoms, the priority was the reduction of the inflammation and spasms in the GI tract, and, of course, a reduction of the pain that was being experienced.

Medical Marijuana, specifically CBD, which has receptors in the GI tract, can be exceptionally helpful with ailments related to the GI tract. A particularly difficult condition to live with is gastroparesis, which is what the patient was suffering from. As the name implies, it is a type of

82

paralysis of the GI tract. Specifically, the muscles in the stomach that move food out of the stomach and into the rest of the digestive tract are not functioning properly. This could be a result of damage to the vagus nerve, which regulates the digestive system. Gastroparesis is often a lifelong condition, with no known cure, although treatment can help.

I knew right away that CBD would be the best bet for the patient. Almost in tears during the appointment, due to the chronic and intense pain, the patient was almost to the point of giving up. When I explained how Medical Marijuana could help, I could see the relief in their face. I explained how CBD has both anti-inflammatory properties and anti-spasm capabilities. The patient understood right away how this natural medicine might relieve the pain they had been experiencing for so long.

Essentially, my first goal, was to calm down the muscle spasms and reduce cramping pain, as well as GI inflammation. The nausea that that was being experienced was probably the result of the GI spasms. Remember the feeling whenever you've had to vomit; it starts low in your belly, and you begin to feel the contractions (GI spasms) building before the stomach compresses forcing the contents up and out.

For daytime use, I prescribed a Low THC - High CBD ratio as this ratio has shown to work best to reduce spasms and inflammation. At night-time, I prescribed a High THC -

Low CBD ratio as this ratio has shown to work best to reduce pain and increase appetite. With this protocol, I was able to reduce the inflammation in the stomach almost immediately. The proof that this was the proper regimen came during the one-month follow-up appointment. The patient was already reporting a reduction in pain and an increase in appetite.

The continuation of the protocol helped decrease feelings of nausea, allowing larger meals to be eaten, resulting in increased body weight. While the symptoms have improved, this does not mean that the patient's gastroparesis is "cured." Bottom line, the patient's quality of life has vastly improved, and that is always the ultimate goal, especially when you're dealing with an incurable conditions.

Keeping a healthy weight is important on both ends of the spectrum. You don't want to carry excess weight, nor do you want to be wasting away. You want to be within a healthy range of your ideal body weight. Many people use a Body Mass Index (BMI) chart, and these can be helpful. The downfall of BMI charts is that they don't necessarily factor in a person's frame and muscle density (Athlete vs. Non-Athlete).

Maintaining a healthy body weight is the key to overall health. For example, women, to maintain their reproductive health, they need about 17 - 20% body fat. Women who are serious athletes can go for months without having their menses as a result of having a very low body fat percentage. This can negatively affect hormone health and balance. In fact, the basic molecular structure of sex hormones in your body is fat-based. So, you have to have enough fat in the body, but not too much. A healthy ratio of body fat to muscle helps maintains general health.

When a person is unable to maintain enough fat or muscle in their body, all of their systems will be affected. This is why the appetite stimulating properties of Medical Marijuana can be exceptionally helpful. Using Medical Marijuana to treat a person is a more holistic approach, as I can address what's happening with that person. All of these things are factored in when I make a prescription recommendation. With my knowledge of how Medical Marijuana functions in the body, along with my background in nutrition, I am able to make a quick assessment of someone's overall health, and determine what a best first THC-CBD ratio would be.

Making Patients Comfortable And Functional!

Chapter 13

Dying with Dignity

As I was going through my records to select case studies for this book, I held my breath when I got to this patient. This was a tough case, as the patient and I both were involved in the 9/11 rescue efforts at The World Trade Center (WTC).

The patient served as a first responder for 9/11, spending months with the clean-up and search for bodies, or rather body parts. They were looking for anything to give to a family; a ring, a necklace, anything that could provide closure.

I have a picture of the patient, with fellow first responders, while they were standing on a pile of WTC rumble doing this work. In the picture, no one is wearing protective masks to cover their face as they work among the highly toxic dust and debris from the collapsed WTC towers. As I look at the picture, I realize that each and every one of them is no longer with us. Nobody could have predicted what the ramifications of the rescue work would be in the future. I too, didn't wear a mask when I ran the Stuyvascent High School Triage Center, just seventy-five yards from the WTC on 9/11.

"Those seen in the below picture are not my patients, but, represent an example of the lack of protective respiratory gear during the rescue effort on 9/11."

NEW YORK DAILY NEWS ARCHIVE VIA GETTY IMAGES

In addition to the first responders, those who were working in the Towers on 9/11, those who lived, worked and went to school near the Towers, have a higher risk for developing World Trade Center related cancers that have been causally linked to the toxic dust and environment in lower Manhattan as a result of the WTC Towers collapsing. According to the World Trade Center Health Program, the top 15 cancers associated with the 9/11 toxic dust exposure are as follows: skin (non-melanoma), prostate, skin (melanoma), lymphoma, thyroid, lung, breast, leukemia, colon, kidney, bladder, myeloma, oropharynx, rectum and tonsil. Within the first few years after 9/11, a rise of cancer related diagnoses among those affected by the 9/11 toxins was seen. A second wave of cancer diagnoses, that appear to have arisen from the exposure to toxins, are now being noted and many are losing their lives.

Most of us know the term, "cancer," but let's take a closer look at what's involved when cancer has been diagnosed. Cancer is the uncontrollable cellular division of the prefix; the prefix is the tissue type. For example, prostate cancer is the uncontrollable cellular division of the prostate tissue. Breast cancer is the uncontrollable cellular division of breast tissue. *So, what causes cancer?*

Our first suspect is genetics. If you have a genetic predisposition to develop cancer, and conditions in your body are conducive to cancer developing, you may develop cancer. Testing can be performed to screen for a variety of cancers, which, in and of itself, won't prevent you from developing that cancer. It can help you realize that you can make changes so that the conditions in your body AREN'T conducive to cancer developing. Factors such proper nutrition, sleep, keeping active, not smoking or abusing drugs, and keeping inflammation at bay are examples of controllable actions that can help reduce the risk of developing cancer.

The second suspect for the development of cancer, is external stressors, where the patient has been exposed to known carcinogens over a long period of time. This chronic exposure irritates the tissue causing normal cells to mutate into cancer cells. For example, if a patient has been smoking for years, this could result in cancer of the lip, lung, mouth or throat, as well as the stomach. By smoking, you are constantly exposing these tissues to an irritant, and that irritation causes the normal cells of those tissues to change into cancerous cells.

My patient came to me, almost 15 years after 9/11, with a diagnosis of sarcoma. Sarcoma is a not-very-common form of cancer that shows up in the muscles, fat tissue and bones. Most of the time, it's not clear what leads to sarcoma, but, exposure to chemicals or excessive radiation may increase risk. Logic therefore suggests that the patient's cancer came from the exposure to toxic chemicals during the clean-up work in 9/11's aftermath.

The patient went through the standard treatment of surgery, chemotherapy and radiation, which can extend a cancer patient's life, and sometimes even save it. Unfortunately, this type of cancer is an especially painful one, as it hits the bones and muscle tissue, aggressively.

The first words the patient said to me were, *"Doc, I'm having so much pain. What can we do?"*

Upon first observation, I noted the patient walked with a cane and had a pronounced limp. During the physical exam, I observed a surgical incision scar as the patient had lost part of an extremity due to a surgical procedure. The person that sat before me was a far cry from the healthy person in the picture shown to me, which I now have, of the patient and other first responders on 9/11. As the patient spoke of the tragedy of 9/11 and of all aspects of the patient's life, I realized this was a truly special individual. The patient had a great personality, which was coupled with an image of strength and stoicism.

We went through all of the symptoms, the pain and discomfort, as well as the prognosis as a cancer patient. After reviewing all the options, we decided to go after any cancer runner cells; these are cancer cells that are hiding and waiting to reproduce and multiply. **Cancer is a sneaky bastard!** It hides, because it wants to survive, just like we want to survive. Runner cells look normal, but eventually turn into cancerous cells. To help achieve this goal, I prescribe an equal THC - CBD ratio. This ratio has adequate inflammation and pain reduction, as well as cancer killing properties.

The patient did well under this regimen for about a year and a half. Upon follow up with the oncologist, the oncologist notified the patient that the cancer had come back and had spread into other organs. The cancer was spreading so quickly and aggressively, that it was almost as if the cancer was angry. The oncologist explained that all avenues of treatment were exhausted. The patient returned to my office and explained to me the poor prognosis. The patient ended with, *"Doc, my time is near. I want to pass on my terms!"* So, I placed the patient on palliative therapy. Not long after, the patient entered hospice and passed away.

Medical Marijuana is not a miracle healing agent. There are certain things that it can help with, and it has been documented to assist with cancer therapies. However, it's not a cure-all. In the case of my patient, as the light dimmed, I prescribed a High THC - Low CBD ratio to help reduce pain and improve the quality of life that remained. The patient was always there for others, whether friend, family or stranger, ultimately, sacrificing their own life, to do the right thing for others. The patient was able to pass painlessly and with dignity.

It was an honor to provide compassionate care for one of our first responders in their time of need. It's always a privilege to take care of someone when they need my help the most. To help my patient's transition, was an absolutely humbling experience, and one that I will never forget.

As an Osteopathic Family Practitioner, I was trained to help patients from womb to tomb. I have experienced the miracle of delivering babies, helping someone navigate geriatric conditions, and helping people transition to death. As much as it hurts to help someone die, it's ultimately comforting because many times that is when a person needs me most.

For those men and women who made the ultimate sacrifice,

> *"May the road rise to meet you. May the wind be always at your back. May the sun shine warm upon your face. And the rain fall soft upon your fields. And, until we meet again, may God hold you in the hollow of his hand."*

9/11: Never Forget!

Conclusion

The Importance of the Doctor/Patient Relationship

How many times have you been to a doctor's office, waited 30, 40, or 60 minutes to see the physician, made to wait in a cold examination room, and then, if you're lucky, get 5 minutes with the doctor? With the emphasis of electronic recordkeeping, I've had patients report to me that the physician barely makes eye contact anymore, since they have to get those notes down, in order to be paid.

Or, have you ever been to see a doctor, and felt that your questions were "**inconveniences?**" Maybe you've been to the physician, complaining of an ache or pain, and that doctor doesn't even touch you to see where the true source of the pain may be.

Most of us place a huge amount of confidence in our physicians. We entrust them with our health, and in some cases, even our lives. As patients, we are vulnerable, and the power balance is often tipped towards the doctor. For this reason, and many more, open communication, mutual respect and trust are critical in a healthy doctor - patient relationship.

But what makes a good doctor? Certainly, most of us have had a bad experience at some point in our lives; maybe a healthcare provider who repeatedly interrupted you, or a physician who dismissed your questions and concerns. Maybe the surgeon who missed a serious problem, or performed an unnecessary operation.

A "good doctor" doesn't come from a piece of paper. I have several pieces of paper hanging on my wall, showing potential patients my training and credentials. Of course, you want to find a healthcare practitioner who has a good reputation, who is board-certified in their specialty, and who stays on top of the research in their field. But, all the pieces of paper in the world won't give a physician a good bedside manner or make him or her truly take an interest in the health and well-being of their patients.

I think trust is of primary importance in any relationship, especially the doctor - patient relationship. When patients are asked what their physician can do to gain and nurture their trust, they point to competence, attentiveness, caring and patience. Patients appreciate a doctor who asks plenty of questions, and who encourage patients to be proactive in their own care, and ask a lot of questions, too.

I spend a lot of time educating my patients, and learning from them, too. I try to laugh with them, and use humor to make my patients comfortable. If a patient looks like they need a hug, I hug them. Let's face it, patients aren't coming to see me because they feel good; they are coming to see me because they are hurting. Sometimes they're coming to my office because they've just been given a terminal diagnosis, and they want me to help them pass on their own terms. These people need my undivided, loving attention, and that's what any good doctor should provide.

I think, just as important as an effective prescription of alternative therapies like Medical Marijuana, maybe more important, is the quality of the doctor-patient relationship. You are reading this book, I am guessing, because you are not satisfied with your current healthcare program or regimen, and that might mean, also, that you are not happy with your current healthcare provider.

If you are searching for a new physician, and are close enough to visit me at my office, by all means, please do! But, I realize that not all of you who are reading this can do that, so I hope that this section of the book will help you find a healthcare practitioner who will truly help you reach your health goals.

Let's start with **communication**. Are you greeted warmly? Does he or she listen attentively? Are you given enough time to communicate your concerns? Are you interrupted often during your visit? Now, I realize that most doctors are pressed for time, but a doctor who rushes you through your visit is dangerous; not only might they make an uninformed decision about what can truly help you, they are also missing out on establishing a trusting relationship with you.

If you feel dismissed, or rushed, or ignored, let your doctor know. You can express this very calmly; "*I'm sorry, I feel a little rushed here….*" or "*I'm sorry, but this is all very confusing, can you re-explain things, maybe a little more slowly?*" If the physician takes this in stride, and helps you out, great! If not, I think it's a sign to start looking elsewhere for a doctor who is concerned with your specific needs.

You have a role, too. Your health is your health, and the **patient's role** is critical. You have to share all your concerns and symptoms, and disclose everything that might be a factor, even if it's a little embarrassing. Your doctor needs to know the entire situation in order to accurately diagnose and help you treat your condition.

As you've been reading this book, you may notice that, in most cases, I discuss treatment options with a patient, and we make a decision together on how to proceed. This notion of **shared decision making,** in my opinion, is critical. If your doctor doesn't give you the opportunity to choose which treatment option you are most comfortable with, they are doing you a great disservice. Your doctor should be your partner, not a dictator. If you feel like a physician is *"pushing you"* to accept a particular treatment plan, push back, or walk away if they are ultimately disrespectful of your input.

I once had a patient who was a healthcare professional, themselves. They were trained in assessing blood work and had extensive nutritional training. When a family member was hospitalized, after suffering hundreds of micro-strokes due to a reaction from a new medication, the family thought they might have lost their matriarch.

Fortunately, the patient survived, and while in the hospital recovering, the patient's regular physician came in for a visit. Relieved to be talking to the physician, my patient asked if they could ask some questions of the physician. *"Sure,"* the doctor said.

My patient had noticed that the calcium levels in the blood work were very low, and knowing that calcium is necessary for proper muscle movement, asked the doctor if this could be related to the weakness that the patient was experiencing prior to the stroke.

The doctor cut them off, mid-question, and said, *"No - that's not important - it doesn't matter."* Calmly, my patient suggested that maybe it might be important, and explained their medical training and background. The physician raised his voice, and said, *"How dare you question my authority. Who are you? I don't even know who you are. I have worked with this patient for 8 years, and you come in here and question my authority?"*

He turned on his heels, and left the room. Everyone was stunned, and looked at each other in silence. An already extremely stressful experience was made far worse by the terrible **bedside manner** of this physician. They changed doctors as soon as they could.

When we are in pain, or anxious, or scared about our health, we are rarely more vulnerable than when we are in that situation. The same goes for our loved ones, who are equally, maybe even more scared. Doctors often have to deliver bad news, or answer tough questions.

A doctor who is arrogant and impatient, or cold and rushed, and who demonstrates any type of poor bedside manner, is no doctor in my eyes. My patient's experience with her family member's physician should never have happened. Here this family was faced with the near-death of their beloved matriarch, and this doctor should have listened to any questions, with patience, empathy and understanding.

You may find a physician that checks all of the boxes: patient, kind, respectful, a listener, and someone who honors your role, as a patient, in the decision-making process.

However, maybe you just don't like them. There is definitely something to be said about being **compatible** and being comfortable. Maybe he or she is just a little too direct for your taste, or maybe they talk too fast, and you can't keep up. Maybe there's just a core personality difference that makes you uncomfortable.

Trust that. Trust yourself. Find that doctor that you enjoy seeing and spending time with. You are more likely to provide that physician the information he or she needs to help you make the best decisions you can about your health.

Other things to pay attention to so that you can find a doctor you trust; look for repeated malpractice claims. Keep in mind, most physicians who have practiced for any length of time will have been sued at one point or another. But, if the physician has a history of lawsuits, that's definitely a red flag, and I would back away slowly, if I were you.

In today's overmedicated world, I think it's important to know about who your doctor might be influenced by. Ask your doctor about drug company representatives and medical device manufacturers that they might work with. Often times these company representatives entice a doctor to develop a working relationship with them by catering lunches, or with other perks.

Listen, no doctor is perfect. I know I am far from it. I try to be the best doctor I can for my patients, but I know sometimes it's not always a great fit. I make mistakes, and I always have a lot to learn. But, as a physician, who truly cares about his patients, I try to make sure that each of my patients knows that I am here for them, no matter what.

No, you will not find a perfect doctor. But, if you take the time to find a doctor who fits what I've described above, you might just find a doctor who's perfect for you.

Knowledge Is Power!

DR. THOMAS G. O'BRIEN II

Acknowledgements

To my parents, Thomas and CaroleAnn, for teaching me compassion and strong work ethics. "Never quit!"

To my sister, Tracielyn Ann (Tra), for decades of encouragement. "You got this Tommy!"

To my wife, my rock, Kathy (Baby Cakes), for making this book a reality, who gave me a family and who believes in me.

To my children, Alexa and Gabrielle, for allowing me to be the best Dad I could be. "Mr. Softy".

To my best friends, Bill, James, Tim, Chris G, Chris Mc and Peter, for years of support. "Re-create myself!"

To Denise, creator of Goddess Project, for developing and maintaining my informative website.

To Bishop Dr. Timothy Birkett, for giving me the opportunity to have my own award-winning television show, " Ask Dr. Tommy O."

To DJ Johnny "Juice" Rosado, for introducing me to Charles "Chuck Chillout" Turner. Public Enemy #1 - "One Take!"

To DJ Charles "Chuck Chillout" Turner, for introducing me to Lenny Green, host of "The Quite Storm" and Dr. Bob Lee, Host of "The Daily Dose".

To both Lenny Green and Dr. Bob Lee, for allowing me to be a guest speaker on their syndicated show, aired on 107.5, WBLS, FM - New York.

Thank you all!

-Dr. Tommy O

Medical Marijuana

In Memory of Professor Ken Jenkins (NCC 1966 -2018):

~ More than a Teacher ~

A mentor, a community leader, and a father figure.

My relationship with Professor Jenkins started over fifty years ago, when I was a young child. He was a tall, soft-spoken man with a clear vision. He knew exactly how to motivate his students. He had an open door policy, allowing his students to ask for help when they needed it the most. After I completed my formal education, I would visit his office twice a year. In mid-August of 2018, I stopped by his office. The office was dark. This was unusual, as his office was always filled with positive energy. I just knew something was wrong, I just didn't know what! As I left his office, I immediately called my father. Now I know, the office was in mourning! What I will miss the most - giving him a Hug and Kiss on the cheek, and having a quick 15-minute conversation.

I Didn't Get A Chance To Say Good Bye!

Dr. Thomas G. O'Brien II, FHS-82, NCC-86

I am proud to have known Prof. Ken Jenkins as a colleague for over 50 years. I knew Ken in many ways and capacities, a friend, a family friend and neighbor to my Mom and Dad, English Professor for my wife Carole, my children Tommy and Tracielyn, Department Chair when I was in administration. I worked with Ken in many special needs programs for Nassau County. Ken was the only one from the college to call Carole to assure her that he was there to help when I had a serious eye accident. Ken and I shared many students. We recommended each other to students, especially students with needs. Ken was a great leader in a quiet way. He guided and mentored students. Ken instilled hope and confidence in ever one he met. Most of all, Ken was son Tommy's other Dad. Ken, thank you for your friendship. God reserved a special place for you! Dr. Tom O'Brien, Prof. Emeritus (NCC 1964-2014)

The quintessential example of a gracious man. He embodied both, intellect and compassion, which helped to mold many a mind, heart and spirit. Kyle Jason

Professor Jenkins was well respected by his students. The life lessons he instilled in his students, including me, were immeasurable. Not only did he provide us with sound academic skills, but he encouraged us to self-actualize and realize our full potential. His method of teaching centered around inclusiveness, embracing students of all backgrounds, and the importance of being non-biased. Christopher McCoy, FHS-82, NCC-86

Prof. Jenkins was very insightful and extremely dedicated to enlightening his students by teaching African-American history that was not given to us in our elementary and high school years. Marc Poussaint

Compassionate Care

Dr. Thomas G. O'Brien II

121 East 60th Street, Suite 4D

New York, New York 10065

(212) 201 - 9122

www.DocTommyO.com

Ask Dr. Tommy O Show:

www.youtube.com/DrTommyO

Health Education Learning Program, Inc.:

www.HELP-10.com

Raised in Ancient and Due Form!

MM

RM

KT

SIMB

Made in the USA
Lexington, KY
04 December 2019